CompTIA A+

certification

Basic Study Guide

By Alfred Quinn

Copyright©2016 by Alfred Quinn

All Rights Reserved

Table of Contents

Disclaimer

While all attempts have been made to verify the information provided in this book, the author does assume any responsibility for errors, omissions, or contrary interpretations of the subject matter contained within. The information provided in this book is for educational and entertainment purposes only. The reader is responsible for his or her own actions and the author does not accept any responsibilities for any liabilities or damages, real or perceived, resulting from the use of this information.

The trademarks that are used are without any consent, and the publication of the trademark is without permission or backing by the trademark owner. All trademarks and brands within this book are for clarifying purposes only and are the owned by the owners themselves, not affiliated with this document.

Introduction

CompTIA A+ is the key to any IT career in the world. This certification is recognized by all companies worldwide, meaning that you will be very advantaged with this certification. However, most students taking this course have complained of it being tough. This has led to some of them failing the exams. However, the reason behind this is the lack of proper mechanisms on how to prepare for the exam. This book guides you on how to prepare yourself for this exam, and how to score a good grade. Enjoy reading!

Chapter 1- Brief Overview

CompTIA (Computing Technology Industry Association) is a non-profit organization whose main focus is to train and certify young and adult IT professionals. The association was created in 1982 and given the name Best Association of Computer Dealers (ABCD). This name was later changed to Computer Technology Industry Association so as to reflect the evolving computer industry. In the 1990s, the association expanded and started dealing with mobile computing, imaging, UNIX, networking, and multimedia. The association usually helps low-income individuals to get relevant IT skills, including computer maintenance.

The certification exams for CompTIA are offered through the Pearson VUE testing centers. The association also provides those interested with corporate membership.

The A+ certification offered by CompTIA demonstrates whether one is competent as a computer technician. It covers various technologies and operating systems for companies such as Apple Inc., Windows, Linux, and Novell. The exam for this certification is usually created for IT professionals having 500 hours of hands-on experience. Each question in the exam has multiple choice answers, and the question might have more than one answer which you should choose from the available answers. For you to receive the CompTIA A+ certification, you have to pass two exams.

The first exam is referred to as "CompTIA A+ 220-901", and this usually covers PC peripherals and hardware, networking, mobile device hardware, and the basics on how to troubleshoot computer hardware and networking components. The second exam is referred to as the "CompTIA A+ exam 220-902," which covers installation and configuration of operating systems such as Android, Windows, iOS, Linux, and OS X. It also covers issues concerning the fundamentals of cloud computing, security, and operational procedures.

Chapter 2- Troublesome Topics

Although the CompTIA A+ exam is easy for individuals to pass, there are some topics which are usually challenging. These might make you fail the exams, hence the need for you to study them extra hard. Here are the topics:

1. Printers

   This topic can be boring to most candidates. You might doze off while trying to read through it. However, even after finding yourself in such a situation, just push on and continue reading. It is recommended that you set some time aside so as to concentrate on printing devices, most especially on how to troubleshoot them. It might happen that your exam will have more questions on this topic, so if you ignore it, it will become a challenge for you to tackle the exam. For you to answer questions regarding this topic, you should have knowledge about both the software and hardware. It is good for you to know how to start and stop spooler service, manage permissions, access the print-que, and once again, be sure you know how to troubleshoot.

2. Port Numbers

You should be aware of the mail port names and numbers before going to sit for the exam. Although it can be hard for you to memorize these, try as hard as you can. However, the good thing about this topic is that only a few questions, most likely jusy one question, is tested from it. However, this is not a guarantee, as you might end up finding more questions from the topic. If you are not prepared for the topic, you will end up failing the exam. Even though it might one question, it might make the different between passing and failing.

3. Windows OS Upgrade Paths

Most people have no interest in reading this topic. A general knowledge about upgrade paths for Windows is of great importance. Most people usually read the path from the XP to Vista, and then Vista to 7, which is not good.

It is also good for you to be aware that, depending on the OS which is to be installed, it might be impossible for you to perform an in place upgrade based on the current Windows version. If the upgrades are not possible, it is recommended that you perform a clean install, but be ready for more work, since you will have to backup the files, install new OS, and then restore the files and the necessary settings. This is good for preparing you for OS upgrades in the company, and this is why you should expect it on your exam. Be sure that you are prepared to tackle it.

4.   Network Configuration

This topic is usually tested in the CompTIA A+ certification exam, and can be challenging to most people. Most of the questions are from the topic of Network adapter configuration. However, this is not hard, but tricky. If you are aware of the necessary steps for doing this, then it will be easy for you, but if you don't know the steps, be sure you study them before the exam. You should also familiarize yourself with the configuration of WAP.

Those are the main topics which usually challenge most individuals. After studying for the 802 exam, it is important for you to ensure that you practice enough. Most people are good in theory, but very poor in practical work. Don't fall under this category. Familiarize yourself with Windows 7, XP, and Vista. There are high chances that you will come across a question asking you about the path to a particular tool or utility for any of the above operating systems, and if it happens that there are multiple answers, you will have no virtual environment in which you can be able to configure it out.

You have to know that the paths usually vary for the three operating systems, so if you have worked on all of these, the better. However, the good thing is that these might be related. This means that if you have worked on one operating system, you can infer the path in the other operating system from what you learned. However, if you have a chance to practice on all of the operating systems, do not hesitate to do it, and you will do better.

It will be beneficial to develop detailed plans on how to study for the CompTIA A+ exam.

Chapter 3- How to Study for CompTIA A+ Exam

Passing the CompTIA A+ exam requires a lot of dedication on the part of the candidate. There are number of mechanisms which you can use to study for this exam. It is possible for you to study for the exam on your own and do well. However, for you to succeed, you have to be highly motivated and possess a strong work ethic.

Most people think that the CompTIA A+ exam usually covers the basics of the computer, and this is what really makes them fail. The exam is not easy, so a lot of dedication is needed when preparing for it. The topics covered include laptops, PC installation and configuration, computer hardware, networking, mobile devices, laptops, Windows operating systems, and security.

Self Study vs. Taking a Class?

One has a wide set of options on how to study for this exam, and they can choose to study on their own or take a class. However, there are a number of factors which determine this.

Let us discuss what is offered by each of the options.

Taking an Instructor-led Class

When you take such a class, you will be advantaged in that the materials used for learning will be up-to-date. The classes will also be focused, and you will work hard towards being focused on tackling the exam. Training classes will also prepare you in advance on how to tackle the questions which you may find in the CompTIA A+ exam. Of course, this will give you a chance to interact with other students learning the same material. These students may ask some questions you have never heard during class time, and this will help you to prepare to tackle the main exam. Other than interacting with students, you will also get a chance to interact with instructors, and once you get used to them, it will be easy for you to ask them any question in case you don't understand something. This will also give you a chance to interact with professionals in the IT field, and you will end up expanding your network.

When you attend an instructor-led A+ class, you will experience hands-on learning. What happens in such classes is that the instructor will come in with old devices such as laptops and desktop computers. These are broken down for teaching purposes, whereby you are shown each part and the purpose of the parts is explained. You are also taught how to assemble these parts. This is of great importance to you as a learner. It has been found that students understand better in hands-on learning than from purely theoretical work. It will also help you learn how to handle your device such as the laptop without fear of damaging it. With such experience, you cannot be compared to students who only studied about these on their own. When it comes to tackling exams, you will be well ahead. More so, you will also be accomplished in the industry.

The problem with instructor-led classes is that they can be expensive for you. For you to get quality training for this certification, expect to pay something in the neighborhood of $2,000. Of course, this is not a small amount of money. Why? We earlier said that the CompTIA A+ certification usually targets low-income earners. However, there are some training centers which will charge something far less than this, so if you cannot afford this, go to the cheaper ones. The advantage with studying for this certification in a quality training center is that you will be provided with extra study materials which will compensate you for the higher price tag, so you will not count it to be a loss. For the training centers charging less, the quality of the training cannot be compared to the ones offered by the higheer charging centers. However, they will also work hard towards equipping you with the necessary skills for tackling the exam and preparing you to work in the industry.

Although it may sound like expensive training centers offer high quality training, while cheaper training centers offer low quality training, this is not a guarantee, as the reverse can also be true. Of course, each center has differentkinds of individuals whom it is targeting for training. These can be classified in terms of social class. The location of the training center greatly influences this. If the majority of those surrounding the training center are rich, then the charges will also be high, and the reverse is also true. This is not a guarantee that the former case offers high quality training, but the charges are set as a result of location of the training center. This is why you have to consider a number of factors before joining any training center, but do not be quick to conclude.

Before joining a training class, it is always good for you to inquire from your close friends. Of course, your close friends might be certified by CompTIA. They can help you choose the best training center for you, depending on what you need. Ask them any kind of question that you may have regarding the best training centers, and they will definitely help you.

However, you should also not fear the high price, since there are numerous benefits that you will get. Entry-level CompTIA professionals usually earn $18-$25 per hour. This should motivate you to pay the fee. Also, once you have paid the high fee, you should be more motivated to work hard to pass the exam. It should make you fear sitting for a retake, and encourage you to work hard for the certification.

You may think that attending an instructor-led class means that you will automatically pass the exam. This is a big lie! You have to do something to pass. Besides what you are taught by the instructor, it is good for you to explore somethings on your own. This is very good, even for increasing your confidence so as to tackle the exam. Don't make attending the class a formality, but go there with an expectation of paying attention and learning as much as you can. There are some individuals who have failed the CompTIA A+ exam despite having attended the instructor-led classes. This is because their concentration was not on learning something from the instructor. Do further research on what you are taught by the instructor.

You should also be dedicated enough in terms of attending the classes. Some people pay for the class, but they end up not showing up, or maybe they attend only for some days. Whatever the instructor teaches is very important for tackling the exam, so it will be good for you to ensure that you always show up. You will get some knowledge from the questions asked by other learners during class time, and this will help you prepare for the exam. However, in case you fail to attend the class, maybe because of an unavoidable reason, it is good for you to follow up and know what they have learned about.

The A+ certification is a stepping stone for you to work with a great company as an IT professional. This is why you see it as an investment for your future, even though you may be paying more for the instructor-led class. The costs of studying it will be outweighed by the benefits.

Self-study

There are individuals who have studied for the CompTIA A+ exam on their own, and they have done well. Although this may not be easy, it is possible. If you have ever worked in a company as an IT professional or maybe you are an IT enthusiast, then chances are likely that you may study for the exam on your own.

However, if you are new to IT, then you have to determine how determined you are. Some individuals like solving problems that they encounter. If you are such an individual, who likes tackling challenges, then the best way for you to study for this certification is through self-study. Try it and it will work out!

Some people are very sure that they are not self-motivated, and that they don't like taking up challenges. If you are such an individual, then this is not the best strategy for you to study for this exam. It is recommended that you attend an instructor-led class. Also, there are some self-motivated individuals who begin a self-study, but things turn out to be tough for them. This usually happens to individuals who have no academic knowledge about IT, or those who have never worked as an IT professional in any company. If this happens to you, do not take it hard, but just join an instructor-led class. The topics covered in CompTIA A+ are very wide, so you should expect to learn a lot. Some people view it as a light certification, expecting to learn something easy, but this is not the case. This is one of the factors which make people fail the exam. Due to the fact that a wide range of topics are covered, the work involved can be overwhelming to you, and learning on your own can be a challenge. This is why you should consider taking an instructor-led class.

Sometimes, it happens that one is not sure of the best way to go. If you are in such a situation, it is recommended that you begin with self-study. This is free, and you will lose nothing other than time, but I am sure that you have plenty of this resource. If the work gets to be too much for you, go for the alternative, which is joining an instructor-led class.

Self-study can be challenging to anyone. However, there are some tips which can help you succeed when doing self-study. Most of these tips have to do with the kind of materials which you are to use and time management. The following tips can help you:

1. Be focused on your end goal- self-study does not involve only studying whenyou feel like studying. There are usually certain expectations and milestones regarding the course that you are taking. The same principle applies to CompTIA A+. You have to achieve the necessary pass mark, otherwise, you will have failed. With self-study, you can study the course in the way

that you want. Always stay focused to achieve more than the pass mark, and all shall well with you.

2. Be wise in time management

Most people practicing self-study will always complain that the work needs much time. You should come up with a clear strategy on how to take care of your family, work, and the self-study program. In school, it was easy for you to manage your time, since you were expected to go to the classroom. However, in a self-study program, no one expects you to do so.

To avoid landing in a problem, ensure that you have a personal calendar. Set a very flexible schedule, and adhere to it. If you need notifications, kindly set and obey them. Once you have studied a particular topic, look for a way to prove that you have understood well so that you can adequatelu prepare yourself to handle the exam.

3.   Reward yourself

Rewarding yourself is one of the best ways that you can stay motivated. Once you have achieved milestones, or after you have earned a badge towards completing the course, it will be good for you to give yourself an incentive so as to keep going. You can forget the studies on one afternoon and have an outing. Eat that cake you have wished to eat! Do what you know can keep you positive.

4. Remember that you are learning

It was easy for you to remember what you have seen, heard, or learned when you were young. This trend is very important in self-study. Whatever you learn in a self-study is expected to change your life and maybe change the entire world. That is why you should keep on reminding yourself that you are learning.

The certification for CompTIA A+ involves two exams. One of the exams is for hardware (220-801) and the other one is for software (220-802). These exams can be taken on the same date, or on different dates, depending on what one wants. It is recommended that one should take the exams immediately after completing the course, since the material is still fresh in your mind, as opposed to taking the exam later.

For those who do a self-study, the exam can be taken individually. However, in such a case, you should first ensure that you have completely read all the relevant materials before attempting to sit for the exam. The funny thing about this exam is that you may encounter some questions for which you find it hard to understand whether they cover the hardware or software. If you have not read the materials well, it will be hard for you to answer such questions. This is why you should ensure that you have read all the necessary materials before attempting the exam.

How to study for 220-801

During the time of study for the exam, be sure that you focus on the following:

1. Disassemble the parts of a computer and printer, and then reassemble them.
2. Identify the different parts of the computer and printer and know their purpose.
3. If possible, set up a small network for your home.
4. Familiarize yourself with networking standards (cables, speeds, Wi-Fi).
5. Familiarize yourself with workplace ethics and OSHA standards.

How to study for 220-802

1. Familiarize yourself with the commands of the command line.

2. Know how to share files and setup groups.

3. Learn more about advanced startup options.

4. Learn more about using admin tools in Windows.

5. Study system requirements and Windows upgrade paths.

6. Do some practice using each of the Windows OS which has been covered (XP, Vista, 7).

With the above tips, it will be easy for you to pass both the hardware and the software exams. Flash cards are very important to you, as they can help you to memorize some information. When learning, it is good for you to write down what you have learned. This will help you in times of review and in memorization of what you have learned. If the task which is being taught can be performed, go ahead and do it. Doing it practically is of great importance compared to just reading it. This will give you much more confidence during exam time, which is a ticket to passing the exam.

Also, it is not optimum for you to rely on a single source of information. When you read the same information stated in different ways in different resources, it will make more sense to you. This will improve the level of your understanding regarding the topics.

You should always remain dedicated. Make sure that you study hard and maintain your goals in mind. You should always set up a schedule and then ensure that you stick to it. Make following the schedule a routine, and the overall work for you will be easy.

Focused preparation

This is a good mechanism for you to prepare yourself for the CompTIA A+ exam. Once you realize that the exam time is approaching, you may find it hard for you to determine the amount of time that you should spend while studying for the exam. Most people think that studying for the CompTIA A+ certification exam for a long time is a guarantee that they will pass. This is not the case.

Total Study Time

Total study time may not be as helpful to an individual waiting to tackle the CompTIA A+ exam, as one might think they have adequately prepared for the exam when they have not. Research has shown that students will only focus for the first one or two hours, after which they lose focus. This means that for the rest of the hours, they will lose the focus, and then the studying will not return any results. Even if you may take 10 hours to read, you will only concentrate for the first few hours, after which you will lose the focus.

Once one's brain has become tired, the individual will just study mindlessly and look for shortcuts. If you find something hard for you, you will easily skip it. Some of the topics in CompTIA A+ are very tough and need a fresh mind so as to be studied. In most cases, once your mind gets tired, you end up skipping reading what is of importance to you. The problem is that you might get used to these bad reading habits with time, and it will be hard for you to avoid in your future studies. Of course, you will not be focused when preparing for the exam, but you will try to get focused when taking the exam, which can't work.

With focused studying, one can achieve a lot while spending very little time. Its focus is to enhance studying while the brain is still fresh. Preparation for the CompTIA A+ certification exam should only take you around 2 to 3 hours. The good thing is for you to read well early in advance so as to avoid reading shallowly during exam time. With this, you will go into the exam room being well prepared to tackle the exam. With focused learning, you will pass your a+ certification exam, and you will not be expected to sacrifice the pleasures of college. You just have to study smart, but not hard.

It might happen that you have not prepared yourself adequately to tackle the A+ certification exam, only to realize that you are expected to take the exam the following day. In such a case, just study for three hours. After that, take your time to relax. Eat and drink what gives your body energy. You can then take two more hours to study and then call it a day. Wake up the next day, and then repeat the same procedure. With such a technique, you will understand whatever you learn rather than staying awake all the night while trying to cram all the notes.

Focused Study Tips

When practicing focused study, adhere to the following tips so as to succeed:

1. Once you have studied for 50-60 minutes, take a break that is 10 minutes long. This is good for keeping your brain fresh.

2. Go to the library.

    Studying in the library is very important, since you will be free from noise. In most cases when you are studying from other places other than the library, you are disturbed by noise from a loud TV, talking roommates, or even the comfort of your bed. After a focused study, spend the rest of the time while socializing with friends. This is because with focused study, you will save some time.

3. Turn off your phone.

Your phone is one of your greatest enemies when it comes to focused studying. This is because you will have instant access to the internet, messaging, and social media apps, which are more attractive than the studying itself. If you feel that these will disturb you, it will be good for you to switch off the phone.

4. Exercise, rest, and eat healthy.

When you combine these three, you will get extra energy, which will help you in focused studying.

5. Utilize your productive time by studying.

Each individual has his or her productive time. This is the time you find yourself focused and determined to do something. Most people find mornings and afternoons to be their most productive times. In most cases, the productive time for individuals is that time when they have more energy. Identify your most productive time and study, even if it is during the night.

Chip Away Strategy

Many A+ exam students have used this mechanism to prepare for the exam and they have been successful. The strategy involves breaking down all the necessary test information so as to get chunks which are more manageable. This strategy should be employed a week before the exam time.

The aim of this strategy is to provide you with a studying strategy which is normal and not torturing. Once you have prepared for the CompTIA A+ certification exam a week in advance, you will just be expected to read for two to three hours each day.

The Study Process

- Day 1- you should spend this day while preparing all the material which is necessary for you to take the exam. This activity should not take more than an hour, so do not spend more than that. This day should just enable you to get started and prepare you for the rest of the days of the week. Do not exhaust much energy on this day.

- Day 2- on this day, the materials should be transferred into a study guide which should cover all of the possible concepts which you can be tested on. With this, you will find it easy for you to know the areas in which you have a low understanding, and get familiar with contents of the materials. This can be done even by transferring your notes from your notebook into a packet which has been stapled. This is also the best time for you to get notes from your classmates in case you had missed a particular class, or to add some clarity to your notes.

Although this one can be your longest day, don't let it take you more than 3 hours.

- Day 3- on this day, you should be focused on the concepts which are hard for you to understand or remember. Sometimes, you might have gone through your study materials without grasping some of the concepts. This is the best day for you to talk to your tutor or classmate who can help you understand these well.

This type of preparation should take you between 1 to 2 hours of your time.

- Day 4, 5, 7- on these days, spend two hours on each of them while thoroughly studying the guide you have prepared. Of course, there are several notes in A+. However, you should have taken some simple notes which you can study shortly, but not all the notes. It is good for you to ask yourself some questions and then speak the answers to the questions out loud. In the next day, write down the answers once you have asked yourself the quiz. If you find that you are right, and then just move on. If you find yourself wrong, repeat until the time you get it right.

During the process of checking, it will be good for you to ensure that you understand the concept very well. In most cases, once individuals have seen the answer, they tend to assume that they will remember it during exam time, and they fail to grasp the content.

- Day 7- on this day, little or no preparation for the exam is expected. This is because it is the exam day. If you feel nervous due to fear of the exam, you can look for the hard topics and then study them for some time. These are the tough CompTIA A+ topics we discussed previously, such as printers and finding Windows upgrade paths. This will make you go to the exam room feeling fresh and very confident to tackle the exam.

Once you follow the above steps for the entire week, you will be far ahead compared to other individuals taking the A+ certification exam. Most of the students usually study for the exam the night before it, and they usually fail. Studying all night for the CompTIA A+ has proved to be ineffective, so you have to come up with a proper strategy on how to study for the exam.

A single night is not enough for you to cover all the A+ certification topics. However, with one full week which has been well planned, you can achieve it. If you study for one night, you will skip some sections, thinking that they will not be part of the exam. You will only be shocked in the exam room to find questions tested on the sections you have skipped. Some people usually try to read the areas they had not read a few minutes before the exam. What happens in such a case is that they end up forgetting everything that they had learned. Passing the exam will become difficult for you.

Also, you will not enjoy sacrificing your sleep so as to study for the A+ certification exam. You will have to do a lot of cramming, and you will build up much anxiety. You will also waste the next few days in sleeping and trying to do away with the anxiety.

It is always good for you to avoid stressing yourself until the results are released. Study with a good strategy on each day, and you will definitely pass the exam. With dedication, individuals usually find the A+ certification exam easy to tackle. However, if you don't prepare adequately for it, things will be tough for you.

Chapter 4- What Next after failing the Exam?

You may have already failed the CompTIA A+ certification exam. This exam is always stressing and very challenging to most people. If this has happened, you will have to consider the money you have invested, and the future of your career as an IT professional. Taking all of these factors into account, you will feel bad after failing the exam.

Missing a passing grade for a certification is not a strange thing, and one can easily find himself or herself in that situation. However, instead of getting discouraged, you can use this to benefit yourself. The following steps can help you once you have failed a certification exam:

1. Do not panic.

Once you have missed the passing grade, you will feel frustrated, disappointed, and discouraged. However, instead of getting panicked, take advantage of the situation to gather the most important thoughts for you, most probably if you are thinking of taking the exam for the second time. Ensure that you have a copy of the exam, together with your results. This will help you know what you scored in the different areas. It is good for you to have a paper with the score, questions, and answers to the specific questions. With this, you will be in a position to know the areas which led you into trouble. If you are planning on taking the exam for the second time, focus most on these parts.

2. Take notes.

Once you have visited the testing center, sit down and make as many notes as possible before you leave. Write down the questions which seemed to be difficult for you, the topics which were most covered, the answers which were challenging to you, and any other thing which seemed to be important to you regarding the exam. The topics which challenged you most in the exam should also be noted down, but you don't have to write down the specific questions and answers.

Also, you should note that before you could take the exam, you agreed not to share information regarding the exam with anyone. This means that the notes that you write are only for your personal use, and not for sharing with anyone.

3. Be focused.

You have to remember that you will not again encounter the specific questions you have just done. This means that there is no need for you to keep on memorizing them. You should only stay focused on the things which left you confused. The notes and the results from your first exam should only act as a guide for you when you are studying. If you have not yet downloaded the exam requirements checklist, make sure that you do so immediately. This should then be used as the master checklist, but if you can't do it, add an effort in your studies.

4.   Use a variety of resources.

Although you may be attending an instructor-led class, make sure that you have access to other sources of information. Although you are provided with original sources of information in class, extra study materials will give you a new and fresh view of the world. Make sure that you have additional books, by checking in your local library. You may find one for yourself which yoou can use for free.

5.   Recuperation.

Exam failure can make you experience negative emotions. Just relax and know that you are not the only one who has undergone this. You are neither the first individual nor the last one to fail the exam, so you don't have to be worried at all. Once you have overcome the negative emotional state, it will be time for you to take a new direction.

Since you have performed below your expectation, it will be good for you to talk about it with your professor. They will likely know what you did wrong in the previous exam, and will help you determine how to study for the future exam and pass it. Although you might be helped by your fellow students, it is good for you to approach your professor, as they have much insight into the course. If you are sure you had studied well, show the professor what you had studied and the amount of time you had spent on each topic. They may end up providing you with information which will help in tackling your future exam.

Seek answers to the following questions:

- Did I study the correct materials?
- Did I prepare myself in advance?
- Did I prepare myself well?
- What else could I have done?
- How did the best students study for the exam?
- Do I have to go to a class again?

6.   Rebound.

Now that you are relaxed enough and have a greater perspective regarding what happened in the past exam, you can begin to rebound.

Be sure that you are aware of the next exam date, and then adequately prepare for it. The following are some of the ways that you can prepare for this:

- Assemble the necessary materials needed during the exam time.
- Use a focused preparation mechanism to get the best outcome from your time.
- Improve the study process by use of the knowledge you gained after talking to the professor and fellow students.
- Try to avoid any mistakes usually made when preparing for the exam.

Your last score should not act to discourage you, but since you have enough information, take it as a way to encourage yourself to tackle the next exam.

7.   Strategies for the next step.

Determine the thing which made the exam tough for you the last time. Ask yourself whether you had enough sleep the night before the exam, or if you had spent too much time while tackling a single question. In most tests, you are provided with an initial block of time which you can spend reading through the questions, and in other cases, you will be provided with a sample set of exams which will help familiarize yourself with the testing procedures which are normally used. This time will not be counted, so take advantage of it to familiarize yourself with the questions, get comfortable, and avoid being tense. The "mark" feature should also be used in the exam so as to help you in saving time.

Sometimes, it happens that you are not 100% sure whether a particular choice is the correct answer to your question. In such a case, just mark it so that you can review the question at the end of the test. You may find a question which is related to this one in the next ones, and this can help you gain some insight into the correct answer to your question.

Mistakes are unavoidable, but it is always good for you to learn from the mistakes. Although failing an exam can make your present day very negative, avoid allowing it to ruin your next day. Learn from the mistakes that you made, and look for mechanisms to improve on that. The grade should be seen as a reflection of what you had studied, but not who you are. More so, CompTIA A+ certification exams are known to very tough, even by the examination body itself, so no need to stress you out.

Chapter 5- Mistakes to Avoid

There are some mistakes which CompTIA A+ students make when studying and taking the exam. Some of these mistakes usually leave one being frustrated. With frustrations, it is difficult for one to do well in the exam. It is easy for one to cope with a situation in which they have failed a question because they had not studied for it. The problem comes when you study well,but you make a silly mistake during exam time. This will be hard for you to cope with. These are the types of mistakes which you should avoid.

They include the following:

1. Showing up late for the exam.

Some people will sleep past their alarms, even during exam time. If you show up late for the CompTIA A+ certification exam, you will have an immediate disadvantage. First of all, only a minimal amount of time will be left for you to take the exam, and if you run out of time, you will be forced to leave some questions unanswered. Although the system for CompTIA might be counting the exam automatically, you don't know the time that your instructor needs to take the exam. Also, when you show up late for the exam, your mind will be anxious, meaning that its performance will be poor compared to when it is calm.

If you do not have any other task, such as attending a class, it is recommended that you show up for the exam at least 10 minutes early. This will even give you time to familiarize yourself with your surroundings such as the furniture and other students.

2.   Stress out.

Having high anxiety will do nothing for you but just hurt you during the exam period. Although you might study all the CompTIA A+ study materials provided to you by your instructor, you may panic when taking the exam, meaning that you will just fail it.

This means that once you stress out, you will do worse in the CompTIA A+ certification exam than your true ability.

This means that you have to look for ways to overcome the anxiety some minutes before the exam. One way of doing this is by writing your values, say 10 minutes before the exam. Yoga is also another mechanism which can help relieve your anxiety. Just stretch and focus on your breathing. With a relaxed brain, you will do very well in the exam.

3.   Skipping a question and forgetting.

As you are aware, some CompTIA A+ certification exam questions are tough, and especially those from the topics considered to be hard. If you come across a challenging question, you don't have to waste much time on it, but just skip it and move on to the next question. You will then come back to the question later. However, this mechanism is only best for you if you have marked, or you use a mechanism to ensure that you don't forget the skipped question. The good thing is that if the exam is taken online, the system will show you the questions which you have answered. However, even despite that, one can forget, especially under conditions of high anxiety.

You can note down the questions which you skip, and this will ensure that you do not forget to answer them. Once you are done with the rest of the questions, ensure that you check where you have noted these questions down, and then answer them.

4.   Failure to answer some questions

This could be as a result of many reasons. You might forget that you had left a certain question unanswered and go ahead to submit the work for marking. This is why we said that you have to answer all the questions. Even if the question turns out to be difficult for you, thete is no need for you to leave it unanswered. The questions for the A+ certification exam have multiple choice answers. This means that instead of leaving any question unanswered, you can take advantage of guesswork and move ahead. With guesswork, you can improve your grade and certainly pass your exam if you could not.

Even in exams with no multiple choice answers, you don't have to leave the question unanswered since you have sufficient question from what you have learned. What about multiple choice answer questions likethe A+ exam? You don't have to leave it unanswered.

For a single question in the A+ exam, there might be more than one possible answer. This means that even with guesswork, you will get some choices right, and this will improve your grade. This is why you should not fail the CompTIA A+ certification exam.

5.   Misreading a question.

This is always brought about by reading the question in a hurry. Some people usually read the A+ exam questions in a hurry, and they rush to read the answers. The questions are usually misread, meaning that you will not be answering the question correctly.

We recommend that you slow down, and make sure that you read the question correctly. The best way to do it is by reading it repeatedly, at least three times. If there is a term which is tough for you to understand, make sure that you take some time to think about it. If you misinterpret it, you will get the question wrongly.

Rushing to answer A+ exam questions usually leads to wrong answers, and people who do this usually fail the exam. Avoid rushing to answer A+ exam questions, but make sure that you first understand the question correctly. This will make you answer the question correctly, and your grade will improve. More so, reading the question repeatedly gives you some time to think about the possible answer to it before beginning to read the ones which have been provided. This means that you will have high chances of getting the question correct.

Questions with diagrams should be observed well. If you don't understand the meaning of the diagram well, then you will get the question wrong.

6.   Changing a correct answer to a wrong one.
Some people like changing answers to questions they have already answered. In most cases, they end up

changing the correct answer to a wrong one. Also, it is possible for you to select the wrong answer when you intended to select the correct one. For instance, it is easy for to select letter "C" rather than the choice "D," and you may not realize that you did that. You should always check to ensure that you have selected the right answer.

This is why you should double check to ensure that you have selected the right answer. Use your fingers for matching the correct answer to its correct choice, and you will answer your questions correctly.

It is always good for you to go with the first selected answer, since there is a reason why you chose it. The first choice is very important compared to the decisions that you make slowly and at a later stage. Note that there is a great difference between making a correction and guessing, so avoid being a victim of the latter case.

7. Submitting the work before checking the answers.

Everybody needs to be done with the exam as soon as possible and forget everything about it. However, it is good for one to check for the accuracy of the answers they have chosen, and this will only take 3 to 5 minutes.

However, do not guess the answers to the questions you had selected, as this will lead you to making some other mistakes. You should just be verifying to ensure that you selected the answer which you intended to select. You should also check to ensure that you had read the question correctly, answer the questions which you had skipped, and make sure that no question has been forgotten to be answered.

8. Running out of time.

You can show up late for the exam, and run out of time. Being slow when taking the exam can also make you run out of time.

Some people usually get stuck on a single question, spending around 5 minutes on it before getting started. Instead of wasting time on that question, just mark it and leave it unanswered and go ahead to answer the ones which are easy for you.

When you continue to the next questions, you may get a clue which can help you to answer the question which seemed tough to you. This means that the best way to handle such a question is to leave it unanswered for a while, and then get back to it at a later stage. Some of the CompTIA A+ exam questions are related to each other, meaning that you can get a clue on how to answer a question from another question.

Sometimes, despite your effort, time may run out before you are through with answering your questions. Most people have complained of the time for taking the CompTIA A+ exam not being enough. What you should do is to ensure that you run after the automatically tracked time by the system. Although it is good for you to care about the time allocated by the instructor, you can use charm and continue doing the exam. Tell the examiner that you are almost finished, and they may grant you some more time so as to finish the exam. This tactic has helped many A+ students to pass the exam. Make the best use of the time to do what you can do to pass the exam.

9.   Forgetting to submit the exam.

Some people will forget to submit the exam once they are done. If you fail to submit the exam, you definitely get a zero, which is a failure. Students doing exams online usually forget to click on the Submit button so as to submit the work for marking. Instead, they just switch off the computer, and the work gets lost. This usually makes them fail the exam.

Chapter 6- Sources of Review Materials

The CompTIA A+ is seen as the starting point for any career in IT. Large companies such as HP and Dell require that their technicians be A+ certified. This is why you should not miss getting this certification. The certification involves two exams, which one must pass. This calls for a thorough review. You have to rely on a wide source of review materials so as to pass these exams. The following are some of the sources of review materials for the CompTIA A+ certification exam:

1. Professor Messer

   This is an IT celebrity who runs a website and YouTube channel of lectures about CompTIA A+. The necessary resources are also provided. The professor has videos of the highest quality, so you will not complain in terms of the quality of sound and pictures in the videos.

This professor has over 25 years of experience in the provision of study materials. The website can be found at www.professormesser.com. You can also visit YouTube and then search for his video tutorials on CompTIA A+. Students who have relied on his tutorials have liked him for his intelligent style of teaching, which has made them pass their exams.

If you like the videos more, feel free to download a portable version, but a small fee will be incurred. However, if you are not interested in downloading the videos, you can just watch them online, and no one will charge you for that.

2.   PC Technician

Online lectures on CompTIA A+ are of great importance. They will help you get a lot of information.

There a lots of sites which offer online practice tests on A+, so feel free to try out these. These will help you to transfer the knowledge which you have learned, maybe in class or through a self-study into practice.

Most of the A+ exam questions have multiple choice answers. You can find such questions online which simulate what happens in a real A+ exam. These are mostly offered for free. Use these as a source of information and for preparing yourself to tackle the real A+ exams.

3. CompTIA A+ Complete Review Guide

Although this source of information is not free, it offers high quality information regarding the same, and this makes it worth the price tag. This one will help right from the time you begin your revies, to the time of sitting for your exam.

It is a book with numerous charts and graphics which help you revise for the computer component modules of A+.

The book has over 500 pages, with about 170 review questions, over 100 electronic flashcards, 4 practice exams and a glossary of key terms which is searchable. This has been included for free, which is an advantage for you, with searching through it having been made a bit easy.

4.   ProProfs Study Resources

Of course, you must have review material which you would like to read constantly so as to avoid forgetting what is necessary for you to tackle the A+ exam. In most cases, these are the sources of information which provide fine details about the course.

ProProfs review materials are an example of this, and they provide you with a means to study the tiny details of the CompTIA A+ course, and these usually make the distinction between passing and failing the exam. This is why you cannot avoid reading these notes. They usually provide you with a quick reference sheet with short points which can help you to tackle your exam. It is good for you to print out this reference list. With that, you will be in a position to read it anytime and anywhere you want.

With the study guide, you will be required to go through a number of slides. Although this can make you feel tired, the information it contains is still useful. With it, you will get all the important aspects of CompTIA A+.

With the over 500 printable flashcards, you will be in a position to identify any gapd in the knowledge that you have of CompTIA A+.

Options exist for either downloading or printing, and with this, you will be in a position to add any review questions of your choice.

5.   Firebrand learn

This is another option where you can all find all study materials for A+. It is free for one to access this online platform, and no one will require you to create an account so as to access it. You just have to visit it and you will get the information directly.

This offers you a great catalogue, and a good platform where you can begin to learn CompTIA A+.

6.   Official Free CompTIA A+ Sample Questions

Some people are not interested in relying on unofficial sources of information. This is because they fear that they might have wrong and unreliable information. This is an official source of communication regarding the CompTIA A+. If you fear unofficial sources of information, then this one can greatly help you.

It is packed with over 1,000 questions, each with an answer and an explanation for the same. These questions cover both exams, for software and for hardware, meaning that no section has been left out.

Once you studied enough of the CompTIA A+ notes, it is time for you to go for these questions so as to test yourself. This will help prepare you to tackle the exam as the exam questions to be found in the final exam will be related to these ones. However, this one is not offered for free. You must purchase it, but the content is worth its price tag.

7.   A+ Certification All-In-One For Dummies

This cheat sheet can be found from dummies.com, and it will provide you with a way to review most of the concepts which are related to Windows such as the recovery tools, boot files, troubleshooting utilities, and RAID types.

8.   Official Free CompTIA A+ Sample Questions

Some of you will not want to pay for the practice exam questions. With this site, you can get a free sample of the practice exam questions. However, you have to provide them with some of your details such as name and email, but there are boxes for deactivating these if you are not interested in provided this information. However, it is good for you to create an account with them as with the email, they can be in a position to update you with news. If they have something new, they will always update you about the same.

After the process of registration has been completed, you will be allowed to access sample questions in two sets, which are for exams, the software and the hardware ones.

9. Study Guides and Practice Tests by RM Roberts

This is a very great study guide which can be found online. In this guide, you will find the exam 220-801 being covered in only domains 1-5 while the domains 1-4 for the exam will be covered. The material is always available, and you can download it for use offline. That is how flexible it is.

10. CompTIA A+ forums

Asking other people for help is always something of great importance. There are numerous online forums from which this can be done. In case you are stuck on a particular CompTIA A+ topic, it will be good for you to ask through these online tech forums. If you speak with instructors and A+ student, you will greatly benefit. Only human beings can be in a position to answer questions which are very tricky. When you check the available online forums, you will save a lot of time.

With those resources, you can adequately review for your CompTIA A+ exams. Make sure that you rely on some of the above resources. You don't have to study all of the above resources, but reliance on a few of them will be good for you.

Chapter 7- CompTIA A+ Exam Tips

The following are some of the tips which can help you pass the A+ exam:

1. Familiarize yourself with CompTIA A+ exam objectives.

    Downloading the exam objectives for the CompTIA A+ is one of the ways to prepare you to tackle the exam. After the download, make sure that you read through them so as to know more about them. The document with these objectives can be downloaded directly from the website.

    This document will teach you more about the exam requirements, and as serve as a guide for you when going through the computer technician program. It should be used as the checklist for one's studies.

2.   Familiarize yourself with the inside parts of the computer.

You should know the various parts of the computer, as well as how to connect them. It is good for you to have a desktop computer. Take apart all of its parts by unscrewing the optical drives and disk drives while observing each of the individual components. This is why you should have a desktop computer which you have preferably set aside for this purpose. You should also familiarize yourself with connectors, components, and how these have been interconnected.

3.   Use study materials available on the Internet.

There are numerous study materials available on the Internet, some for free and others are for sale. We have discussed these in our previous section. Although the course comes with all notes necessary for you to pass the exam, it is also good to rely on additional sources. Sometimes, you may fail to understand some of the topics discussed in the course content. This call for you to research the topic, and only the sources available on the Internet can help you. Some of these resources include videos, tutorials, pictures, and others, and these will help you gain additional knowledge about the course, meaning that you will have high chances of passing the exam.

4.   Take practice exams.

The course for computer technicians has been developed with unit quizzes, reviews, and an exam after completion of a major section. It is good for you to review these sections so as to ensure that all is well. Once you have reviewed the quizzes, it is good for you to go through them for practice. Both the midterm and the final have also been developed so as to provide you with practical experience. The midterm can be taken as many times that you need while the final can be taken up to a maximum of 3 times. There are several sites online from which you can find practice exams about A+. You should visit these websites and do the necessary practice.

If you are to take the main exam the following day, make sure that you eat energetic food, have a good sleep, develop a positive attitude, and arrive in the exam room with some minutes to spare. It is always good for you to schedule the parts of the exam on the same day.

5.   Read the PBQ questions.

CompTIA provides us with some descriptions, reviews and questions on

https://certification.comptia.org/testing/about-testing/performance-based-questions-explained.

You can access these and read them thoroughly. You should be sure that you will find these questions as the first ones in the main exam. Know the actions which are needed for you to answer these questions, and then apply the same concept in the main exam. You will definitely pass it. When reading through these questions, do not view it as if you are wasting your time, but do it with confidence. This should be the first step before you can schedule your test.

6.   Skip PBQ questions which seem tough to you.

If you find a PBQ question or maybe the multiple choice question is tough to you, just look for a mechanism to mark it and then move on to the next question. In CompTIA exams, one is allowed to mark the tough questions for reviewing them later. One is only allocated 90 minutes to do the PBQ questions. This is why you don't have to spend much time on any of the questions, The PBQ questions are always tough, so if they happen to be difficult for you, skip and review it later, but ensure that you have marked it to avoid forgetting.

The good thing with the CompTIA A+ exam is that it has multiple choice answers, and if you are very familiar with the technical niche, it will be easy for you to answer the question correctly. This is because you are just expected to find the correct answer and then select it.

7.   Identify the phrase or keyword which has been used in the question.

In each question that you find in the CompTIA A+ exam, there must be a keyword which has been used, and this is what confuses people in most of the cases. It is after this that you should look for the best answer to pair with the keyword. We always recommend that you familiarize yourself with the vocabulary for CompTIA A+, and you will find it easy for you to answer the questions.

8.   Know the reason why some words in the questions have been capitalized

In most cases, the word which has be capitalized carries the main meaning of the question or it is where the trick lies. If you don't realize this, then chances are that you will get the whole question wrong.

9.   Use elimination.

The A+ exam usually involves multiple choice answers. If you have read the course content well, or if you have good knowledge in the IT niche, it will be easy for you to use the elimination method to answer the questions.

Once you have read the question and understood it very well, identify some of the choices provided in the answers which cannot be the answer and do away with them. Your aim should be narrowing this down so that you can remain with few answers to compare. With this mechanism, it will be easy for you to get the right answer for the question, as opposed to when you have to compare all the answers which have been provided for the question.

10.   Create logical deductions.

This is another mechanism which can help answer the questions effectively. With logical deductions, you just have to break down the answers and the questions. In fact, this one will make the process of elimination simple for you. Reduce until you are left with a minimum number of answers possible for comparison. You will end up getting it correctly.

11.   Know the wrong answer.

With the knowledge of the wrong answer, it will be easy for you to get the correct answer. This is because you can easily apply the elimination method. If you know the wrong answers, just eliminate them until you are left with a few choices to compare. You will then know that a particular choice has the highest probability of being the answer compared to the rest. This way, you will get it right.

With this, you might not have read much, but you may end up getting the question correctly. This even becomes much easier for you if you have a great knowledge about the CompTIA A+ course.

12.   Anticipate the answer when reading the question.

It is good for you to think of what the answer should be when reading the question. Does this before you can read the answers which have been provided? This means that once you have read the answers, it will be easy for you to know the correct answer. However, this calls for adequate preparation for the exam, as when you have not prepared well for the exam, you will not be in a position to anticipate the answer. This will also save you from doing guesswork, which may cause you to get it wrong.

13. Take advantage of later questions to answer future questions.

We said that once you find a tough question, use the marking mechanism and leave it unanswered. Instead of wasting too much time on the question, just skip it and move on to the next question. The good thing is that you may later find a question which will give you a hint about how to answer the previous question. If you get a hint, it is good for you to note it somewhere, or go back immediately to answer the question before you can forget. This will ensure that you get most of your questions correctly, and you will have high chances of passing the exam.

14.   Avoid leaving blank answers.

There is no reason why you should leave any question unanswered, simply because you don't know the answer to it. Try all the methods we have discussed to get the answer to the question, or maybe the approximate answer to the question. You have to know that an unanswered question in CompTIA A+ equals to a zero. There is no reason for you to leave the question unanswered, especially if you had some preparation for the exam. If the above methods fail to work, just guess the answer. The question might need you to select more than one answer, meaning that you have a high probability of getting at least one answer correct if you guess. Guesswork has helped most students to pass the exam. Even if you get all the answers of a question correctly, you will get some correct, and this will boost your grade. Note that a guess may mean a pass or a fail in the A+ exam.

15. Avoid changing your answers anyhow.

Some people always try to change around answers when taking the CompTIA A+ exam. This is not recommended. There is a reason as to why you chose the first answer. After changing the answer, you will regret doing so, and in most cases, immediately after the exam, because you just changed the answer from the correct to the wrong one. Avoid falling a victim to this. We recommend that you stick to the first answer, unless you are sure what you are changing to is the correct answer. If you are guessing, avoid it, but stick to the initial answer.

16. Take both exams on the same day.

Some people like to schedule the two exams on different days. However, this is not good, and not recommended. You should take the two exams on the same day. The knowledge you get after doing the first exam is necessary, and can help you greatly when taking the second exam. The two exams are related, and this is the reason behind this. If you schedule both exams on different days, you will have forgotten what was in the first exam when taking the second exam. This is why the two should be taken on the same day.

17.   Be confident.

If you lose confidence, you will fear the exam, and you will definitely fail. For you to be confident with what you are doing, you have to prepare yourself well for the exam, and in advance. This calls for a thorough review of the exam.

You have to be sure that you will pass the exam. If you doubt yourself, you will find it difficult to think while taking the ComPTIA A+ exam. Most of the questions are tricky, and these require a confident, sober mind to tackle. Prepare yourself to gain that confidence, and all shall be well.

Conclusion

We have come to the conclusion of this guide. If you follow the tricks discussed in this book, you will pass the CompTIA A+ certification exam, and not only that, but you will get a very good grade. For this to happen, you have to prepare yourself very well for the exam. However, this doesn't mean that you study all day and night for the exam. No! You have to come up with a nice strategy on how to study for this exam, and you will make it. There are numerous study mechanisms which have been discussed in this book, so adhere to them and you will get a good grade.

The good thing with the CompTIA A+ is that you can choose to do self-study or attend an instructor-led class. The choice depends on what you want. Of course, for an instructor-led class, you have to pay for it. This is the reason why most people choose to do self-study. If you have a good IT background, self-study will suit you, but this doesn't mean that you should not take an instructor-led class. Even after starting self-study and then things turn out to be tough for you, do not hesitate to join an instructor-led class, as it is never too late for you.

You should know that CompTIA A+ is the key to your career in IT, so don't waste your time and other resources while studying for this certification. Large companies such as HP and Dell will always want you to possess this certification so that they can employ you as a computer technician. The common mistakes, such as showing up late for the exam and leaving some questions unanswered should be avoided by all means.

www.ingramcontent.com/pod-product-compliance
Lightning Source LLC
Chambersburg PA
CBHW061017050326
40689CB00012B/2671